What's My Purpose?

A Journey of Personal and Professional Growth

By Jim White, Ph.D.

What's My Purpose?

A Journey of Personal and Professional Growth

Copyright © 2007 by JL White International, Inc.
Published by JL White International, Inc.
457 Webster Street
Monterey, California 93940
(T) 877-647-3103 (F) 831-656-9423
www.whatsmypurpose.com
www.jlwhiteinternational.com

What's My Purpose? is a trademark of JL White International, Inc.

First Edition
Printed in the United States of America

Paperback ISBN: ISBN-13 978-0-9795216-0-7, ISBN-10 0-9795216-0-2
eBook ISBN: ISBN-13 978-0-979516-1-4, ISBN-10 0-9795216-1-0

Book Cover Design by Foster Covers
www.fostercovers.com

Table of Contents

Introduction and Agreement

When you ask the question, "What Is My Purpose?", you embark upon a journey of personal and professional growth. It is a rewarding yet difficult journey.

You will be asked tough questions throughout this workbook. If you are to benefit fully from this process, you must have the utmost personal integrity in and for yourself. Will you commit to completing the work and exercises thoroughly and honestly?

If you take the process I disclose in this workbook seriously, you will discover things about yourself that lead to significant changes in your life. Some of the people that have completed this workbook have been known to quit their jobs, change careers and receive promotions. Some have moved to other parts of the world. Still others have married or divorced.

The process I lay out in this workbook is extremely challenging. Though you will complete all the exercises that follow and the book will come to an end, your growth will continue for the rest of your life.

If you are willing to face yourself at this intimate level, I will support you in your journey.

Committed To Your Purpose,

Jim White, Ph.D.

I Agree to the Terms of this Agreement.

_____   _____

Name   **Date**

Acknowledgements

There are so many people that have influenced this body of work. I do however want to acknowledge and say thank you to my wife, Lauren, for her unwavering support and love! Thank you, My Darling.

To all my clients who have supported me and trusted in me for all these many years. What a wonderful journey we have shared. Thank you.

Assessment

Now that you have signed your contract, please complete the following assessment.

T	F	Please check the appropriate box, true or false.
☐	☐	1. I sometimes feel that there is something missing in my life.
☐	☐	2. I don't feel much joy in my life.
☐	☐	3. I don't enjoy what I'm doing for a living, but I don't know what else to do.
☐	☐	4. There's something I've always wanted to do, but I can't find the courage to do it.
☐	☐	5. I believe I could contribute more than I do.
☐	☐	6. It seems like I spend my life doing what I "should" do instead of doing what I believe is right.
☐	☐	7. I don't ever seem to have any time for myself; I'm always busy.
☐	☐	8. I can relate to the song that asks, "Is That All There Is?"
☐	☐	9. I have all the things that are supposed to make me happy except I'm not happy.
☐	☐	10. I often compare myself to others, which makes me feel bad about myself.
☐	☐	11. I wonder if being successful is really worth it.
☐	☐	12. It's hard for me to relax; I feel like I need to be doing something all the time.
☐	☐	13. I think about the questions: "Why am I here?" "What's My Purpose?"

☐	☐	14. I believe that there has to be more to life than what I've been experiencing.
☐	☐	15. I try to make things happen rather than allowing them to happen.
☐	☐	16. I am reassessing my spiritual beliefs.
☐	☐	17. I feel like there is something I am "supposed" to be doing, but I'm not sure what it is.
☐	☐	18. I want to make a difference in the world.

Part 1

What Is Purpose?

In the book, "Atlas Shrugged," one of Ayn Rand's main characters is asked, "What is the most depraved kind of human being? His answer would likely surprise most people, since he doesn't suggest a murderer, or rapist, or other sex offender. His answer is, "The man without a purpose."

When asked about why she suggested this as opposed to the other possibilities, Rand replied, "Because that aspect of their character lies at the root of the cause of all the evils which you mentioned in your question. Sadism, dictatorship, or any form of evil, is the consequence of a man's evasion of reality. A consequence of his failure to think. The man without a purpose is a man who drifts at the mercy of random feelings or unidentified urges, and is capable of any evil, because he is totally out of control of his own life. In order to have control of your life, you have to have a purpose----a productive purpose."

Randy Gage, *Accept Your Abundance*

What Is Purpose?

Every once in a while you meet people who are inspired by their work. They exude enthusiasm. They appear to care genuinely about what they are doing, the people with whom they work, and the people they serve. They express a joy that seems to come from deep within; it's not forced or superficial. You sense their genuineness and authenticity, and you don't believe they are playing a role.

When you meet such a person, you realize that their work is consistent with their purpose. You might say they are working "on purpose". They know why they are here and they know the difference they want to make. This clarity and focus on their purpose makes them stand out from most of the people you meet.

Who Are These People?

They could be anyone—a teacher, parent, executive, artist, sales clerk, mechanic, carpenter, social worker, or administrative assistant. It doesn't matter what they do. What does matter is that they do it from a central purpose.

Job satisfaction and fulfillment come from the inside out, not the other way around. For example, two teachers appear to be doing the same thing, yet one has a job, while the other has an impact on children's lives. One feels stressed and burned out much of the time, while the other feels excited, energized and challenged. The difference between them is that one teacher is fulfilling his or her purpose, while the other is doing a job.

Now an Opportunity...

Take 3 minutes now and think of people in your life who seem to love what they do. Write down the names, (or jobs if you don't know the names), of three of these people. Next, describe what it is about them that makes you think they know and live their purpose.

Person #1:
Description of what about them makes you think they know and live their purpose:

Person #2:
Description of what about them makes you think they know and live their purpose:

Person #3:
Description of what about them makes you think they know and live their purpose:

What the Dictionary Says About Purpose

Merriam-Webster's Collegiate Dictionary defines purpose this way:

"¹**purpose**   **a :** something set up as an object or end to be attained : INTENTION

b : RESOLUTION, DETERMINATION **2** : a subject under discussion or an action in course of execution"

"²**purpose** to propose as an aim to oneself"

A Definition

Mission, vision, vocation, calling, bliss, meaning, passion, these are just some of the words that convey our human need to identify and express purpose. Ultimately, finding your purpose is a spiritual quest. It represents your ability to connect with something greater than yourself.

The question," Why Am I Here?" goes much deeper than what career is best for you. This workbook will help you look inside yourself for your answers, which is the only place you will ever find them.

Passion

When you break the word "passion" down, you will find the essence of what purpose is about. PASS-I-ON. Isn't that what you want to do? Do you want to make a difference in the lives of others and leave something of yourself behind? None of us want to think that we have lived and died without leaving any trace of our uniqueness behind.

The word "passion" is also used because it represents feeling. To fulfill a passion is to express deeply held feelings. Passion is not an intellectual or rational brain function; passion comes from the heart. It is a calling.

You don't think about what your purpose is, you feel or know your purpose. You don't figure it out, you experience it.

Passion implies desire. And your passion, if given a voice, will arouse you to take action. Once known, it demands to be fulfilled. If we fail to listen, we suffer stress, fatigue, frustration, or dissatisfaction.

Passion is compelling; it creates an inner sense of urgency, quite distinct from the external events of our lives.

Passion allows us to be truly alive.

Worksheet

Now that you have thought about people you know who are "Working On Purpose" and have read the ideas of others on purpose, what are your ideas about purpose?

What words or phrases would you use to describe it?

To Me Purpose Is:

Symbolizing Passion

You might think of a passion as a burning desire, which is one reason why a flame is often used as a symbol.

Sometimes it is easier to symbolize your passion than to try to describe it in words. Symbols are often richer and more vivid than words. They also speak to the right side of the brain, which is where you experience passion.

There are many reasons for choosing the flame as a symbol. A fire gives off warmth. When you are around people who are living their passion, you notice that they are warm. You can feel them reach out to their work and the people around them.

A flame is also bright with light. When you live your life from your passion, you too are a source of light. Throughout the ages, light has meant truth, wisdom, and knowledge. All of these are appropriate to a life lived with purpose. To follow your passion is to live your truth, as you understand and experience it from the inside. Many people try to live the truth of their parents, friends, or images that they see in the media. Living someone else's truth can only lead to dissatisfaction.

A fire is consuming and powerful. When you know and live your passion, you find that it can consume you. Ironically, that's the goal. George Bernard Shaw expressed it well when he said,

> "I want to be thoroughly used up when I die...life is no brief candle to me. It is a sort of splendid torch which I have got hold of for a moment, and I want to make it burn as brightly as possible before handing it on to future generations".

And your passion is powerful! What is more powerful than the person who has a mission in life? Gandhi, Joan of Arc, and Martin Luther King were empowered by their vision. The depth of their vision inspired and empowered others.

Have you ever stared into the flame of a candle or a fire? You can easily become hypnotized by its flicker. After a time, everything else disappears from your awareness and you seem to merge with the flame. This unity, or sense of oneness, is a reminder of the spiritual experience in which you are no longer separate from the world. When you are in complete alignment with your purpose, you will have a similar experience of oneness.

If the flame goes out, if you feel disconnected from your passion--you'll probably say you feel "**burned out**". You can experience stress from time to time because you become sloppy in your living habits. But if you are burned out, you are probably living from the outside-in. When that happens, your aliveness, your life force, feels snuffed out--dead. However, when you act consistently with your purpose, it's like adding fuel to the fire!

As you work through this book, be aware of pictures, images or symbols that come to mind for your passion. You will be asked to create a symbol for your purpose before you finish this workbook.

Purpose or Meaning?

Is there a difference between these two words? Yes, there is an important distinction. You can have a meaningful life, whether or not you believe you have a purpose.

Meaning is the significance that you attach to an event, person, or situation. You can have meaningful work, no matter what you do, if you decide to assign meaning. To ascribe meaning is a rational left-brain act. A well known story makes this distinction clear:

> Two stone masons were at work when a visitor came upon them. Curious, the visitor asked the first one, "What are you doing?" He replied, "Cutting a stone." Then the visitor asked the second stone cutter the same question. The stone mason's reply was, "I'm building a cathedral." The second man had given meaning to his work.

Purpose is quite different. You do not bestow purpose. It is something that flows from deep within you. Purpose is the potential that you hold, much as the acorn holds the potential for an oak tree. Purpose is what you're called to do. It is a part of your uniqueness. Purpose is your expression of the divine.

Purpose or Meaning?

Purpose and Meaning are both important. Think about what gives your life meaning. Make a list of the people and things that are meaningful to you and why.

People and Things That Are Meaningful to Me	
People/Things:	What They Mean to Me:

Your Most Meaningful Experiences

Think back on your life and recall your most meaningful experiences.

What happened? Why was that event important to you?
What impact has the experience had on your life?

Experience #1:

Experience #2:

Experience #3:

Write Your Purpose/Mission

First Draft

Before you go any further, write down what you believe your purpose is. It is okay to be vague at this time. It will become clearer as we work through this process.

My Purpose Is:

Why Find Your Purpose?

From the time you are born until the time you die, you are growing and changing. As you go through life, there are specific developmental tasks you need to complete before you move on to the next stage. You are probably familiar with the developmental tasks of childhood and adolescence. When you reach adulthood, it's easy to think you're through with these tasks. Of course, you recognize that there will be changes; marriage, children, career moves, empty nest, aging parents, retirement—and SOON. But you may not have related these external events to your internal, emotional, psychological, and spiritual growth.

Midlife, roughly from your late thirties to your late fifties, is the developmental stage at which you need to come to terms with the meaning of your life. Carl Jung was one of the first psychiatrists to write about this period of life. He said,

> "Among all my patients in the second half of life, that is to say over thirty-five, there has not been one whose problem, in the last resort, was not that of finding a religious outlook on life – this, of course, has nothing to do with a particular creed or membership of a church."

The largest segment of our population today is in midlife, the baby boomers. Record numbers of them are asking:

- Who am I?

- What do I want to be when I grow up?

- Why am I here?

- If I'm so successful, why aren't I happy?

These questions are critical if you want to continue to grow toward self-actualization and these questions are uncomfortable. Do you know people who have had an affair, bought a sports car, or found some other way to distract themselves from these questions? Have you been avoiding these questions?

Is Your Present Work Your Purpose?

Answer the following questions Yes or No:

Y	N	
☐	☐	1. Do you love what you are doing?
☐	☐	2. Do you find it easy to work these days?
☐	☐	3. Do work and leisure time sometimes seem the same?
☐	☐	4. Do you feel things are all right in the world?
☐	☐	5. At times, when you feel frustrated or irritated with a particular aspect of your job, do you maintain a deep feeling that what you are doing is still "right"?
☐	☐	6. Do you feel there's nothing else you'd rather be doing?
☐	☐	7. Do you feel at peace in your life?
☐	☐	8. Do you trust that things will work out for you?
☐	☐	9. Do you have a positive attitude most days?
☐	☐	10. Does your work energize you?

Discovering Passion

The cultural dynamics of the eighties and nineties created a sense of urgency around developmental tasks, unprecedented in the history of human development. These two decades were characterized by people living from the outside in, the opposite of following their passion. Money and what it could buy, became equivalent to success. Did you get caught up in this shallow definition of success? If you did, then you may feel that your life is like a lifesaver; there are many things, activities, and people, swirling around the outside, but there is a hole in the middle. Your center—*your passion*—is empty. Joy and happiness can be found when you fill up your center.

Do you know people who hate their work? How did they get into that work? Often, they didn't follow their passion. They let themselves be talked into it because it paid well, was close to home, or had good hours. All of these are important considerations ...*"after you know your purpose."* If they are the only questions that guide your decision, you may find yourself unhappy and dissatisfied with your life.

It is important to note that your passion may not always be what you get paid to do. Your passion might be raising your children, for example, and you may need employment to support them financially. In this situation you might choose a job that is close to home and pays well. Working supports your passion; it is NOT your actual passion. If you can keep this clear, you won't expect your paid work to provide fulfillment and you won't be disappointed. On the other hand, you can make the work meaningful and bring joy and contentment to your life.

Each yes answer on the worksheet "Is Your Present Work Your Purpose?" (Page 25), is an indication that your work and your passion are in alignment. When you answer YES to all the questions, you are living your PASSION.

Part 2

Your Five Masks

Your Five Masks

Mask 1—Busy-ness

Mask 2—What Will Other People Think?

Mask 3—I'm Not _____ Enough.

Mask 4—Fear

Mask 5—The Having Mode

When you put on a mask you are trying to conceal or hide something. Let's say you are going to a masquerade ball, the goal is to conceal your true identity. If you are exceptionally nice to someone, you may be masking other feelings towards them.

You can also wear masks to conceal something from yourself. That's what often happens with your passion – it is hidden from you by certain masks that you wear. In this section of the workbook, you will learn about the five masks that may be concealing your passion. You may discover that you're wearing all five; or maybe you wear only one. Until you can take off your masks, you may be unable to answer the question "What's My Purpose?"

Mask #1: Busy-ness

"The challenge to find meaning in what you do is at the core of the new work ethic. Employees want more than just a paycheck from their work. They want to feel connected to their organization's mission and vision. They look toward the organization as a place where they can grow and accomplish their own personal vision as well as the organization's larger purpose."

Cynthia Scott and Dennis Jaffe, *Take This Job and Love It*

Take a few minutes now to answer the following questions.

How Busy Are You?

1. How many hours do you work in an average week?_____

2. Make a list of the outside commitments you have. Include professional, social and community commitments.

3. Did you choose to work during a scheduled family activity in the past month? For example, did you work on a day when your son or daughter was playing in a soccer game or any other game or event?

4. When was the last time you had an hour alone with yourself with no demands?

5. Do you have all the latest time saving devices? For example, do you have a PDA, a cell phone, etc.?

6. Do you ever feel things are happening too quickly?

7. Do you feel guilty if you aren't doing something?

8. What would you like to be doing if you weren't so busy?

9. Do you feel like you're too busy?

10. Do you need to check your calendar before you can agree to do anything?

What Do You Enjoy?

You may be so busy that you don't take time to do the things you enjoy. It's easy to fall into automatically doing what needs to be done, what you committed yourself to yesterday. A steady diet of this and you begin to lose touch with the things that bring you pleasure and joy. Life can come to feel like a lot of have-tos instead of want-tos. If you have forgotten what you love to do, it will be harder for you to identify your passion. Let go of some of your busy-ness and take the time to record the things that you enjoy.

Worksheet

Make a list of at least five things you enjoy in each of the following categories and then add any other category you wish.

Sports/Recreation
1.
2.
3.
4.
5.

Outdoor Activities
1.
2.
3.
4.
5.

With Friends

1.
2.
3.
4.
5.

With Family

1.
2.
3.
4.
5.

Alone

1.
2.
3.
4.
5.

Your Category
1.
2.
3.
4.
5.

How often do you do the things you enjoy? Weekly? Monthly? Yearly? What excuses do you make to yourself for not doing the things you enjoy? If you don't take time for the things you've listed, you may go after thrills and excitement instead. Unfortunately, excitement is an addiction that gets harder and harder to satisfy. Enjoyment is deeper and more abiding.

What Are Your Talents?

We each come into this world blessed with specific talents and gifts. These are abilities we have that seem to come naturally. These gifts can be a clue to our purpose, in that they can help us fulfill whatever it is we believe we are here to do. These talents could be athletic abilities, dexterity, musical talent, taste, artistic abilities, a sense of humor, comfort with numbers, and so on.

Take time now to think about what your talents are. This is part of what makes you unique as a person.

Worksheet

List at least five talents below.

My Talents Include:
1.
2.
3.
4.
5.

Did you have trouble with this exercise?

Many people cannot identify five talents. They may never have taken the time to think about their talents, or they may not want to brag or boast. Don't worry. To acknowledge and own your talents will not send you on an ego trip. Quite the contrary! Without this basic self-awareness, you cannot make much of an impact on the world.

You may minimize or ignore your talents because they come easily to you. You may assume that if it's easy for you, it's easy for everyone. This is a way you diminish yourself and mask your passion. If something comes easily to you, this is a clue that it is one of your talents.

Other People's Impressions of Your Talents

If you could not write down at least five talents, then this next exercise will help you jump start the process. (Even if you did identify five talents, do this exercise anyway because it is so rewarding and affirming).

Now think of five people who know you very well. Arrange a time when you can speak with them alone without being interrupted. Then ask them these questions:

- What do you think makes me special?

- Do you think there is anything about me that is unique?

- What are my talents?

Then listen and write down the answers they give you.

Worksheet

Name 1 _____
List five talents:
1.
2.
3.
4.
5.

Name 2 _____

List five talents:

1.

2.

3.

4.

5.

Name 3 _____

List five talents:

1.

2.

3.

4.

5.

Name 4 _____

List five talents:

1.

2.

3.

4.

5.

Name 5 _____

List five talents:

1.

2.

3.

4.

5.

My Composite List of Talents

After you have interviewed five people, look over all your notes and make a composite list. Write down the comments that are similar. Do the talents you listed match the list your friends gave you?

Composite List of Talents:
1.
2.
3.
4.
5.

What Are Your Skills?

Now that you have had a chance to think about your talents, let's take a look at your skills.

A skill is something you have learned to do. What competencies do you have as a result of training, experience, or education? Some ideas are: using computers, fixing an automobile, organizing activities, operating heavy equipment, or time management. Most people have dozens of skills. Write down the skills you know you have. Then look at the list on the next page. It may trigger other skills you have and forgot to list.

A Skill Is Something You Learned To Do—Your Competencies.

My Skill List:
1.
2.
3.
4.
5.
6.
7.
8.
9.
10.

You may discover that some of the traits you listed as talents are included on your List of Skills. This is because people often try to develop skills in areas where they do not have talents. For example, some people have a talent for organization. It is a gift and seems to come naturally to them. Other people have worked hard to learn organizational skills by taking workshops, reading books, or by participating in on-the-job training. You will need to make a judgment call about whether the traits listed are skills or talents for you.

List of Skills

Domestic

- ☐ Cooking
- ☐ Cleaning
- ☐ Budgeting
- ☐ Shopping
- ☐ Gardening
- ☐ Decorating
- ☐ Repairing
- ☐ Raising Children
- ☐ _____
- ☐ _____

Recreational

- ☐ Golfing
- ☐ Swimming
- ☐ Hiking
- ☐ Reading
- ☐ Music
- ☐ Crafts
- ☐ Painting
- ☐ _____
- ☐ _____

Self-Management

- ☐ Relaxing
- ☐ Positive Thinking
- ☐ Time Management
- ☐ Imagination
- ☐ Visualization
- ☐ Follow-through
- ☐ Initiating
- ☐ _____
- ☐ _____

Business

- ☐ Organizing
- ☐ Planning
- ☐ Managing
- ☐ Delegating
- ☐ Leadership
- ☐ Speaking
- ☐ Training
- ☐ Writing
- ☐ Accounting
- ☐ Decision-making
- ☐ Strategy
- ☐ _____
- ☐ _____

Interpersonal

- ☐ Listening
- ☐ Assertiveness
- ☐ Asking Questions
- ☐ Motivating
- ☐ Selling
- ☐ Persuading
- ☐ Establishing Rapport
- ☐ Negotiating
- ☐ Problem-solving
- ☐ _____
- ☐ _____

Risk Taking

- ☐ _____
- ☐ _____

Merging Your Talents and Skills

Is there any relationship between your talents and your skills? Have you developed skills that build on your gifts? You may have natural athletic abilities but have you developed any specific skills like those used in tennis? Perhaps you have a gift for writing. Have you developed skills in your use of language? You can make maximum use of your talents by developing skills around them. Your unique blend of talents and skills is a clue to your passions.

In the chart below record your list of talents and the skills you have developed around them.

Talent:	Skills I Have Developed Around This Talent:
1.	
2.	
3.	
4.	
5.	
6.	

Remember the story about talents? Don't bury your talents but instead cultivate them. This may mean you need to develop some skills to take your talents into the world. The more you use your talents, the more you will discover that life flows easily. You can let go of the struggle!

Prescription for Busy-ness:

Cultivate Solitude

> "The creative person is constantly seeking to discover him/herself, to remodel his/her own identity, and to find meaning in the universe through what he creates... His most significant moments are those in which he attains some new insights, or makes some new discovery; and these moments are chiefly, if not invariably those in which he is alone."
>
> Anthony Stone, *Solitude*

If busy-ness is preventing you from knowing your passion, what can you do about it? You can cultivate solitude. Instead of complaining about how busy you are and how you don't have time to do the things you want to do, focus your energies on creating time for yourself.

Creative geniuses have always required and cherished time alone. Creativity cannot emerge when your mind is cluttered with busy-ness and business. Your greatest thoughts and ideas will come in times of quiet reflection and stillness. This is a key to uncovering your passion. Remember, your purpose is not something you can think through and figure out. Instead, it is something that you feel and experience. It comes from deep inside of you.

Imagine yourself trying to talk on the telephone while a jet flies overhead, a rock band plays at a party next door, and a child cries next to you. It would be difficult, would it not? And so it is with hearing your purpose. Your life may be so busy that it drowns out your inner voice. You don't need to make this inner voice louder. It is already perfectly clear. You need to turn down the volume in your life so you can listen to your inner voice.

How can you cultivate solitude? Solitude is not something that you do once a year! Ideally, you need some quiet time every day. During times of transition or when you need to make important decisions, you may need longer periods of solitude. There are many ways to accomplish this.

Listed below and on the following pages are some of the most common ways to achieve solitude. Read through each one and put a check in the box if you could make this a regular part of your life.

☐ Walks

Every day, take a walk alone or silently with another person, for at least 20 minutes. During this walk, focus your attention on the present moment. Try to breathe slowly and deeply. Notice the trees, flowers, and the feel of the wind on your skin. What color is the sky? What is the temperature? Use each of your senses to help you stay in the present.

☐ Journal Writing

Each day, record how you feel and what you are thinking about. There are many ways to keep a journal. One of the best ways is to write everything down, just let it flow. For a journal to be most valuable, you want to record the process and flow of your life, not just the contents. In other words, don't just list the day's events; address the significance of each event, your feelings about them, or your reaction to them. If you don't interpret events, you will miss the great potential of journal writing as a means to self-discovery. It doesn't matter if you use notebook paper, a blank book, or a special journal format. What is important is that you do it on a regular basis.

☐ Meditation

There are many types of meditation, but they all have some elements in common. One method is to spend 20 minutes once a day, sitting quietly, allowing your mind to grow still. You will usually have a word (called a mantra) on your breath as a point of focus. As you direct your attention, other thoughts will gradually drop away. When you begin practicing meditation, you will notice yourself going through several stages. First, you will find it is difficult to quiet your mind. As you learn to do this, you will notice that you can manage your stress better. You will feel calmer and more centered. As you continue in your practice, you will discover more about yourself and become increasingly aligned with your purpose. Meditation is also one well-known path to spiritual growth.

☐ Reflection

It is so easy to lose sight of your life in the midst of living it. Alan Laekin coined the phrase, "What is the best use of my time right now?" to help people manage their time. You may want to use the same technique. Create a focusing question to help you stay on purpose. Here are some possibilities:

- How am I making a difference?
- Is what I'm doing right now on purpose?
- Is this what I really want to do?
- Am I following my passion?

You may need a cue to remind yourself of one of the focusing questions. One way to do this is to go to an office supply store and buy a package of colored adhesive dots. Place these dots in several different places in your office and at home, where you are likely to see them. Then, whenever you see a dot, stop for 60 seconds and reflect on your life, use one of the above questions or others that you create. If you don't like the answer you give yourself, you may need to make some changes.

☐ Quiet Time

This is time, usually spent by yourself, when you eliminate outside distractions. Turn off any music and the television, ask family and friends not to disturb you, and turn off the phone. In this atmosphere of quiet, you can do any personally satisfying activity— sewing, exercising, taking a bath, shooting baskets, watching the sunset, tending the garden, or working on a hobby. Quiet time gives you an undistracted opportunity to think.

☐ Retreats

In times of transitions, you may need more solitude than usual. Some transitions you expect, such as marriage or a job change. Others come as a surprise, such as an accident or a death. When you reach one of life's changing points, it can help to have some extended periods of solitude. A night or a week away may be just what you need. Many people find that a retreat, which allows them to be outside in nature, is more healing than if they were confined to an indoor space.

Retreats are usually most effective when you go alone. However, it is also possible to go with someone and decide, in advance, that you will be silent with each other for a certain part of the time. You might be silent from the time you wake up until the time you have dinner. Just as we sometimes need to clean our closets of accumulated clutter, we also need to cleanse our minds with silence.

It is very easy to fill your life with activities, to be busy all the time. You may even be praised and admired by others for all you can do. But busy-ness can never lead you to your purpose. That's an inside job. Solitude balances the busy-ness with time for you. How willing are you to listen to yourself? Can you know your passion until you do?

Mask #2: What Will Other People Think?

Your first obligation is to carry out the purpose you are meant for, not what your father, mother, partner or friends say you should do. Your mission will manifest in you when you decide to listen to your heart's desire.

Worksheet

In the space provided below, write down what you secretly think you would really, really like to do.

Why aren't you doing it? Could it be that you're worried about what other people think?

Too often, people know what they want to do, but hesitate to do it because of what other people might think. How often do you, before making a decision, ask yourself what someone else will think of the decision? *There is a difference between consulting with someone to get their opinion and consulting to get their approval.* The latter can paralyze you. If you try to please all of the other people in your life, you will discover that it is not possible. It's not very fulfilling either!

Take a moment now and ask yourself who the other people are in your life that you try to please.

Whom I Try to Please:

Are You Pleasing Yourself?

Now think back over decisions you have made in the past month. Did you make any of these decisions based on what someone else would think or did you make them to please yourself? Be very frank with yourself!

Decision #1:
How I Felt:

Decision #2:
How I Felt:

Decision #3:
How I Felt:

The Tyranny of the "Shoulds"

If you look carefully at each of the statements you wrote down on the prior page, you will see that hidden within each of them is a *Should*. You are probably well aware of how damaging *Shoulds* can be to self-esteem. They lead to feelings of guilt, inadequacy, and blame. You may even have invested time and energy releasing some of your *Shoulds*. Nonetheless, people rarely recognize the enormous power that *Shoulds* have to control their behavior and self-perception. More often than not, there is a *Should* between you and your purpose, between you and self-acceptance, and between you and peace of mind.

There are three layers of *Shoulds*:
- Having
- Doing
- Being

Here are a few examples of each.

Having:
>   You *Should* have …
>   a nice car
>   a good job
>   money in the bank
>   the latest fashions

Doing:
>   You *Should* …
>   act your age
>   volunteer in the community
>   learn to swim
>   listen to the news

Being:
>   You *Should* be …
>   perfect
>   strong
>   smart
>   successful

You may have already let go of the Having *Shoulds* and perhaps even some of the Doing *Shoulds*. You might even be tempted to skip over this section, thinking to yourself that you've heard all of this before. But, have you let go of your Being *Shoulds*? These go so deep that you may not have questioned them. Yet they form the criteria upon which you judge yourself and decide whether or not you are okay.

Despite the pains and limitations that Being *Shoulds* impose on your life, they are extremely difficult to let go of. Why? Because they were forged when you were a very young child, and they are now part of how you define yourself.

They provide a formula, although an often impossible one, for acceptance. The terror associated with releasing them is this:

> Who are you if you are NOT your Being *Shoulds*?

To let go of your Being *Shoulds*, you need to take responsibility, in the most profound sense of the word, for YOURSELF.

Shoulds will limit and constrict your life. But more importantly, they can <u>kill your spirit</u>. If you should "act your age" (Doing *Should*), will you ever be able to go to an amusement park and delight in the rides? If you should "be responsible" (Being *Should*), can you ever take a risk? If you should "be modest" (Being *Should*), can you accept your gifts and talents?

Worksheet

What are your *Shoulds*? Include Having, Doing, and Being, but pay particular attention to your Being *Shoulds*.

My Having *Shoulds*:

My Doing *Shoulds:*

My Being *Shoulds:*

When you let *Shoulds* guide your life, you are living from the outside-in, instead of from the inside-out. In other words, you allow these external forces to have control over your life. You give them the power to define you, thereby, they have the power to decide whether you think you are okay or not. It gets very complicated when the people in your life don't agree with what you should do. No matter what you decide, you suffer feelings of guilt, inadequacy, and unhappiness because someone thought you should do something else.

The only way you can be happy is to determine what you believe is right and to behave in a way that is consistent with those beliefs. You may not always please others, but you will please yourself.

Most importantly, when you live inside-out, you are able to follow your purpose, rather than someone else's notion of what you should do. Your brothers and sisters may have worked in the family business, but if you feel called to study art, you will be happier and make a greater contribution if you listen to your calling rather than trying to placate the family *Shoulds*.

Connecting to your higher self, your spiritual self, requires releasing your *Shoulds* and doing the hard work of knowing yourself. Are you ready to let go of your *Shoulds* and replace them with something that will serve you better?

Prescription For Concern About What Other People Will Think:

Determine Your *Values*

As the *Shoulds* fall away, you will replace them with *Values*. **Values are beliefs that you choose to guide your life.** The key word here is <u>choose</u>. *Shoulds* are absorbed without conscious choice. *Values* guide you in separating right from wrong in situations. When someone tells you what you should do, you can check his or her *Should* against your *Values* and decide what is right for you.

Not everyone will share your *Values*. Do you judge people when they hold a different point of view? When it comes to *Values*, there is no right or wrong, good or bad, there is only different. As you stop judging yourself, you will stop judging others. When the judging is silenced, you will be able to hear, with increasing clarity, what it is you really, really want to do.

Most of us can say in a minute what we should do, but it's far more difficult to articulate what we *Value*. Look back over your list of *Shoulds*. Are any of them *Values* for you? Write down in the space provided any *Shoulds* that actually reflect *Values* you have. To shift your *Shoulds* to *Values*, you will need to change the way you talk to yourself. Instead of saying, "I should do volunteer work", (which creates guilt) try saying, "I choose to donate time to community service". Other words you can use to replace your *Shoulds* are "I want" and "I prefer".

Worksheet

SHOULD	VALUE

All the *Values* you have as an individual make up your personal *Values* system. You may have fooled yourself into thinking you behave according to your *Values*. In fact, many people find that it is extremely difficult to do what they believe is right, especially when faced with opposition. Here's an example, you may say you *Value* time with your family, yet you agree to work overtime whenever you are asked, because you "*Should*" be a team player. To be truly led by *Values*, demands integrity and responsibility. Rather than taking a stand for their *Values*, most people slide back to listening to their *Shoulds*. You can guarantee against this by being clear with yourself about what you do *Value*.

Values Clarification

Listed on the next page are different *Values*. Rank how important each one is to you on a scale of 1 to 10, with 10 being most important to you. Then rank your behavior—how well you LIVE your *Value*, using the same scale of 1 to 10. Use the blank spaces to record any *Value* you hold that is not listed. If the numbers in the first two columns are more than 3 points apart, use the action step column to write down the action steps you need to take to bring your behavior and your *Values* into alignment.

Values Worksheet

Value	Importance	Behavior	Action Steps
Achievement			
Aesthetics			
Affection			
Altruism			
Appearance			
Arts, Music, Etc.			
Authority/Power			
Autonomy/Personal Freedom			
Career/Employment			
Community			
Creativity			
Emotional Health			
Environment			
Expertise			
Family			
Home			
Honesty			
Integrity			
Learning			
Leisure Time			
Love			
Loyalty			
Meaning			
Money			
Openness			
Personal Growth			
Physical Health			
Pleasure			
Privacy/Solitude			
Recognition			
Relationships			
Religion			
Risk Taking			
Security			
Service			
Socializing			
Spiritual			
Status			
Trust			
Wisdom			

As you went through the list, did you notice that there are some *Values* to which you assigned a low ranking, yet much of your behavior is directed toward those *Values*? That is a clue that *Shoulds*, instead of *Values* are controlling your behavior. People often commit their time, energy, and resources to activities that are not in alignment with their professed *Values*. For example, you might have ranked Service as low, yet you serve on committees in your community and on other boards. When someone calls looking for volunteers you say, "yes"!

Your resources, time, energy and money are limited. Remember that when you say "yes" to something, you are saying "no" to something else. Clarifying your *Values* helps you make wise choices and escape the tyranny of the *Shoulds*. Saying "yes" to your passion means saying "no" to your *Shoulds*.

Select Your Most Important *Values*

Select six (6) most important *Values* from your list on the preceding page and give an example of that *Value* in action during the past week.

Here's an example:

> *Value*: Honesty

>> "When my husband asked if I would like to go out for pizza, I told him the truth and said, 'I'd rather stay home'".

Value #1:
Example:

Value #2:

Example:

Value #3:

Example:

Value #4:

Example:

Value #5:

Example:

Value #6:
Example:

Did you have difficulty with this exercise? Until you put your values into action, you won't be able to create the life you want. When your behavior is in alignment with your *Values*, you earn Integrity.

Replace *Shoulds* with *Values*

Some of the *Shoulds* on your list may not reflect your *Values* at all. In fact, they may be in direct opposition to your *Values*! One of the best ways to let go of *Shoulds* is to replace them with *Value* statements. Look back at the list of *Shoulds* you developed earlier. Some of them were, in fact, *Values* that you converted by changing your language. But the other statements do not represent what you believe. Record them in the left-hand column of the table below. In the right-hand column, write down the *Value* you want to live by. You will need to decide for yourself which *Shoulds* are not *Values*. See the example below before you begin.

Example:

Should	Value
I should spend time on the weekend with my relatives.	I want time alone on the weekend.
I should buy a new car.	I prefer spending my money on travel, rather than on transportation.
I should make a certain amount of money.	I want to do meaningful work regardless of what it pays.

Worksheet

I SHOULD	VALUE I WANT

This process has just helped you eliminate meaningless *Shoulds* and unnecessary guilt. You have made an active choice about what is important to you and what you believe. Now, when someone pulls a *Should* on you, you can check their *Should* against your *Value*. If there is a match-Great!

Change the *Should* into a choice and feel the increased sense of personal power. If the *Should* does not coincide with your *Values*, let it go and refocus your *Values*. This will free you from Mask #2—"What Will Other People Think?".

Value Conflicts

Sometimes you may have two *Values* that seem to compete with each other. You then need to decide which of the two is more important to you. These are usually difficult choices. Imagine that security is a high value and so is service. You may work as a volunteer, providing services to the needy in your community while your partner works at a high-paying job. This arrangement allows you to honor each of your *Values*, without conflict. But suppose your partner is laid-off and cannot find employment? Then what happens to your *Values*? You may find yourself in conflict between your service and your security *Values*. You will need to choose which *Value* is higher for you. There is no "right" answer. There is only your answer.

The only time you can compromise a *Value* is for a higher *Value*. For example, you might *Value* loyalty and truth. What would you do if your boss asked you to do something that you believed was deceitful? If you compromise your *Values* for any reason, other than a higher *Value* (because it would be easier for example), you will lose your self-respect. It is not long after that, that you lose self-esteem.

Value conflicts are painful. They demand that you go deeper into yourself to find your own truth. They can be internal, interpersonal, or cultural. Look back through your list of *Values*. Are you experiencing any *Value* conflicts? Write them in the space provided.

Worksheet

Internal Value Conflict

Example: Do I work on the book manuscript this evening (Meaningful Work) or spend time with my partner (Family/Relationships)?

My Internal Value Conflicts:

Interpersonal Value Conflict

Example: Do I express how I'm feeling (Honesty) and risk being excluded (Sense of Community)?

My Interpersonal Value Conflicts:

Cultural Value Conflict

Example: Do I landscape my yard like other homes where I live (Aesthetics/
           Relationships) or do I save money for my child's college fund
           (Family)?

My Cultural Value Conflicts:

How have you resolved these dilemmas for yourself? Are you still struggling with some of them? The ultimate solution to a *Value* conflict is contained in the following Paradox:

Paradox: The only way out is through.

Create or React?

This all boils down to "Who will be in charge of your life?". Will you create the life you want, a life that is consistent with the *Values* you hold? Or will you allow others to control you with the *Shoulds*? If you do the latter, you will spend your time reacting and responding to what others want, never completely satisfying them or yourself. If you are not in this mode you have a greater chance of fulfilling your individual purpose. And isn't that why you are reading this workbook?

Now, I want you to write down what you think you really, really want to do.

Worksheet

What You Really Want:
I want

Mask #3: I'm Not _____ Enough

"Everyone has his/her own specific vocation or mission in life to carry out, a concrete assignment which demands fulfillment. Therein, he/she cannot be replaced, nor can his/her life be repeated. Thus, everyone's task is as unique as is his/her specific opportunity to implement it."

Victor Frankel, *Man's Search For Meaning*

Meaning

Are you beginning to realize that with each mask you are peeling off, you are also seeing the ways you have stopped yourself from knowing or fulfilling your purpose? This third mask addresses how inadequate we can sometimes feel when we try to meet what we're called to do. In what ways do you feel you're "not enough"?

I'm Not ...

_____ Enough

_____ Enough

_____ Enough

_____ Enough

More often than not, you feel as if you are not enough when, in fact, YOU ARE ENOUGH! Remember the story *The Wizard of Oz?* The Tin Man, Scarecrow, and Lion were all seeking something they didn't believe they had. A funny thing happened when they got to Oz and met the Wizard. They each discovered that they already had what they were seeking. They hadn't acknowledged it. Is it possible that you too have all that you need?

Worksheet

In the spaces provided, think of three situations in which you were "enough". It might help to think of times you believe you made a difference in some way.

I was "enough" when:

I was "enough" when:

I was "enough" when:

Now look back at how you filled in the blank, "I'm not _____ enough."(Page 68). In any of the three situations you just wrote about, did you have enough of *that something* that you think you lack?

The Comparison Trap

Sometimes you don't feel "enough" because you're comparing yourself to someone else. The comparison trap is very seductive because sometimes you "win." In other words, sometimes you come out smarter or more talented or better in some way. Unfortunately, you usually lose and feel inadequate, or less than, the other person.

Worksheet

Look again at how you are "not enough" and ask, "Compared to whom?"

I'm Not _____ **Enough**

Compared To: _____

I'm Not _____ **Enough**

Compared To: _____

I'm Not _____ **Enough**

Compared To: _____

I'm Not _____ **Enough**

Compared To: _____

What did you discover? Are you making comparisons? The sooner you stop comparing yourself to others, the sooner you will be on your way to knowing and living your passion. A belief that you're not "enough", or not adequate, is an indication of self-esteem. To let go of Mask #3, you will need to raise self-esteem.

Prescription For Concern About What Other People Will Think:

Develop Self-Esteem

Self-esteem is how you feel about yourself. You either like yourself or you do not. If you do not like yourself, it will be very difficult for you to trust yourself enough to listen to your inner voice which will tell you what your passion is. If you do listen to yourself with low self-esteem you probably won't risk acting on your knowing. You won't feel you are "worth it".

In Mask #1 you were asked to list your talents and skills. Very often people with low self-esteem have difficulty identifying their talents. They find it hard to believe that they are unique. Was it hard for you to list your talents?

Self-Esteem Inventory Worksheet

Please read the following statements and answer each True or False.

T	F	
☐	☐	1. I can admit a mistake.
☐	☐	2. I can reach out to people I don't know.
☐	☐	3. I maintain my values even when other people do not approve of them.
☐	☐	4. I can accept a compliment without feeling uncomfortable.
☐	☐	5. I can be myself around other people.
☐	☐	6. I accept myself with all my faults and weaknesses.
☐	☐	7. I can tell you my strengths.
☐	☐	8. I can feel joy for someone else's achievements.
☐	☐	9. I do not compare myself with others.
☐	☐	10. I have peace of mind.
☐	☐	11. I believe I am unique
☐	☐	12. I can let my inner child out and play without worrying about what others will think.
☐	☐	13. I accept differences in others without judging them.
☐	☐	14. I affirm myself and others.
☐	☐	15. I openly express my love for others.
☐	☐	16. I love myself.
☐	☐	17. I accept all my feelings
☐	☐	18. I enjoy my own company and I am comfortable being alone.

The more Trues you have, the higher your self-esteem. If you have less than 13 Trues, you may want to build your self-esteem using the exercises that follow.

Self-Talk

You talk to yourself all day long. In fact, you are talking to your self right now! During these internal conversations, you may be planning, worrying, rehearsing or remembering. As you engage in these thoughts, you might also be judging yourself. For example, if you're planning, you may think, "I don't know how to do this; I'll never figure it out." If you're remembering, you might think, "Why did I say that....it was a stupid thing to say." Or perhaps you are worrying with thoughts like, "I bet I don't get the promotion because I'm not as experienced as the other candidates." It is these judgmental thoughts that cause feelings of low self-esteem. What you say to yourself will effect how you feel about yourself.

For the next day, pay attention to your self-talk. In the space provided, jot down what you say to yourself, and then carefully review it.

My Self Talk:

Keeping a self-talk log is similar to keeping a time log or a food journal. It lets you see in writing what you are saying to yourself. Once your self-talk is on paper, you can analyze it for *Shoulds*, judgments, and other negative thoughts. Reading what you've written down can bring a painful awareness.

Yet, until you know what you are doing, it is not possible to change. After you become aware of how you judge yourself, you can move to the next step, which is to say "Stop!"! When you catch yourself starting to judge, with some practice, you will become very good at blowing the whistle on yourself and replacing the judgment with positive self-talk.

Daily Acknowledgements

How often have you gone to bed at night rehashing in your mind the mistakes and the errors in judgment you made or the words you spoke that were better left unsaid? When you do this, you erode your self-esteem. To increase your self-esteem, try giving yourself a daily acknowledgement instead.

A daily acknowledgment consists of taking a few minutes before you go to bed to recount to yourself 10 things that you did that you feel good about. These do not need to be grand accomplishments! The quality of your life is measured by the little things. Reflect back over the day for all the positive things you said or did. If you fall asleep remembering the things you feel good about, you will awaken feeling good about yourself.

The following example of one person's daily acknowledgment will help you with the kind of things to include. Take a moment right now to write out your daily acknowledgement list for today. You can add to it tonight, if you like. The following page can be photocopied for you Personal Daily Acknowledgement List. At the end of each week, review your daily acknowledgements for the entire week— all 70 items (10 per day)! As your list grows, your self-esteem will grow!

Example List of Personal Daily Accomplishments:

1.	I got out of bed when the alarm went off.
2.	I took time to pet the cat before I left for work.
3.	I kissed my partner goodbye and said, "I love you"-with feeling.
4.	I let 3 people merge into my lane while I was on the freeway driving to the office.
5.	I returned 2 phone calls without procrastinating.
6.	I said, "thank you" when the mail carrier dropped off my mail.
7.	I gave someone my full attention when I listened to him or her.
8.	I turned the TV off when the show I wanted to watch was over.
9.	I ate an apple for desert instead of cake.
10.	I hung up my clothes instead of draping them over the chair.

My Personal Daily Accomplishments

1. _____

   _____

2. _____

   _____

3. _____

   _____

4. _____

   _____

5. _____

   _____

6. _____

   _____

7. _____

   _____

8. _____

   _____

9. _____

   _____

10. _____

   _____

Your Uniqueness

As you gain clarity about your purpose, you will discover that it has a synergistic effect on your self-esteem. Once you realize you are here on a mission that only you can perform, you will find there is no need to compare yourself with anyone else. Everyone has a unique mission to fulfill. Each person will fulfill his or her purpose using his or her personal set of talents and skills. How and where you use your gifts to fulfill your purpose will depend upon your personal life experiences. No one else on the planet is exactly like you.

As you raise your level of self-esteem and love for yourself, you will come to know yourself better and to know what makes you unique. This knowledge will help you fulfill your personal purpose. You will bring to bear all of your life experiences-good and bad, all of your talents, all of your skills, and all of your hopes to make an impact on the world.

Take some time to reflect on the following questions. Use what you have discovered so far about your skills, talents, and values to help you. If you do not have an answer now, it's okay (but dig deep when you are looking for answers). Let yourself absorb the question over time and the answer will emerge.

Worksheet

1. How am I unique?

    _____

    _____

2. What skills and talents make me unique?

    _____

    _____

3. How have I used my uniqueness to affect my world?

    _____

    _____

4. How does my personal set of life experiences enable me to make a difference in the world?

    _____

    _____

5. When have I made a difference?

    _____

    _____

6. How did I do it?

_____

_____

7. Is that a clue to my uniqueness?

_____

_____

8. When have I felt most alive, energized, and present to the unfolding of my life?

_____

_____

9. Deep in my heart, why do I believe I'm here?

_____

_____

Paradox: The question is the answer.

Affirmations

Another strategy you can use to build your self-esteem is that of giving yourself affirmations. This is the final step in the process of changing your negative self-talk. The first step was to become aware of what you say to yourself with the self-talk log. Then you practice interrupting the thought with the word "Stop!". The second step was to record your daily acknowledgements, focusing on the positive instead of the negative. Now you will construct positive statements, or affirmations that will eventually replace your negative self-talk.

With an affirmation, you affirm (in the present) some time you want to create in your life in the future. Remember, you are today who you thought you were yesterday! In other words, if you've been telling yourself you will never find the right job, you are probably working right now at something you don't find fulfilling. If you continue to think the same way, you'll continue to get the same outcomes. However, you can change this pattern if you change your thinking. If you start today to affirm that you have meaningful work (assuming you don't already), you create that outcome for yourself in the future. Napoleon Hill was right when he said, "If you think you can or you think you can't, you're right".

Make statements to yourself that reflect the life you want. As you make these statements, keep in mind these rules for affirmation:

Rule #1: State Them in the Present Tense

Your behavior tends to mirror what you believe. When you state something to yourself as if it were true today, your behavior will come into alignment with the belief more quickly than if you state it as being true in the future. For example, if you are looking for a new job, you will not get as positive a result by saying, "I will find a good job" as you would if you affirmed, "I have the job I desire."

Rule #2: State Them Positively

Your mind can work more effectively with affirmations that express what you want, rather than ones that express what you don't want. For example, "I accept myself" is more powerful than, "I don't criticize myself."

Rule #3: Use Them Every Day

As you know, you talk to yourself all day long. Your affirmations need a chance to be heard in the midst of all the negative self-talk. Say them frequently, at least every morning and every evening. If you say your affirmations as you fall asleep at night, you will be programming your subconscious mind when you are relaxed and more susceptible to suggestions.

Rule #4: Empower Your Affirmations with Feelings

When you say your affirmations to yourself, evoke as much feeling as you can. This is like supercharging your affirmation. You remember things that you feel. Recall a favorite movie or book. You probably remember it because it touched you on a feeling level. Express your affirmation with feeling and you will create it faster!

Your affirmations can be about anything. You might start with affirmations related to your self-esteem. The more you like yourself, the more you will trust yourself and the more likely you are to share your gifts with the world. Below are some sample affirmations. Use them as a starting point, then write your own. You will want to start with no more than two or three. As you bring these into reality, you can add others.

1. I now accept myself.

2. I am everything I need.

3. Every day, in every way, I am growing more and more healthy.

4. Let go of the negative thoughts.

5. I am a loving person.

6. I love and respect all of my natural abilities.

7. I am a patient person.

8. I have achieved all my personal goals.

9. I have the quality of life I want.

10. I have the house of my dreams.

Worksheet

My Personal Affirmations:
1.
2.
3.
4.

Now check what you have written against the four rules for affirmations. If you need to make any changes to what you wrote, do so now.

As with Daily Acknowledgements, you will begin to notice a difference after about one month of using affirmations. You will be pleased with the results.

I Am Coming To Realize That My Purpose Is...

Mask #4: Fear

With the other three masks removed, you have now reached the fourth reason why you may have hesitated to follow your heart. Are you afraid? There are two kinds of fear associated with your passion. First, you may be afraid to know what your passion is. Why? Because once you know, you are confronted with your responsibility to take action to follow your passion. You can allow yourself to be passive only as long as you "don't know" what you want to do. Most people want to be in control of their lives, yet few want to accept the responsibility that goes along with it, and they use fear to avoid knowing. Could this be true for you? Are you afraid to know the truth?

The second kind of fear occurs after you know what your passion is. This is the fear that is associated with taking a specific action toward fulfilling your passion. For example, you might need to go back to school and you may be afraid to do so. In the space provided, write down as many of your fears as you can think of. Be as honest with yourself as you possibly can.

I Feel Afraid to Fulfill My Purpose Because...

Types of Fear

Most fear falls into one of these five categories listed below. Look at the fears you listed and put them in to one of these categories:

Failure.

Being laughed at, not doing it right, not knowing what to do, making a mistake, not being capable.

My Fears of Failure:

_____

_____

Success.

Being overrun with success, losing friends because of it, overworking or becoming a workaholic, gaining notoriety, having too much responsibility.

My Fears of Success:

_____

_____

I'll Get Hurt (physically).

The stress of it will make me sick; it might kick up my ulcer; I'll have a panic attack; I won't be able to breathe.

My Fears of Getting Physically Hurt:

_____

_____

I'll Get Hurt (emotionally/psychologically).

They won't like me, I'll be rejected, I'll be excluded, I'll be embarrassed, I won't be able to cope, I'll make a fool of myself, my mate will leave me.

My Fears of Getting Emotionally/Psychologically Hurt:

_____

_____

The Unknown.

I don't know what will happen, I don't know what to expect, I won't be able to cope with what happens, I won't know what to do.

My Fears of the Unknown:

_____

_____

Understanding Fear

Fear is an uncomfortable feeling. Consequently, people often try to hide their fear or to overcome it. But, like any other emotion, fear doesn't respond well to these tactics. It works better to understand and befriend the fear. How do you do this? You begin by recognizing fear as soon as it arrives. To do this, recall one of the fears that stopped you from doing what you really wanted to do. Once you have the feeling in mind, answer the questions that follow.

Where Do You Feel the Fear?

For example, fear lives in some people's stomach. When they get the sensation of butterflies in their stomachs, they know it is present. For some, it lives in their legs. The expression knee-knocking describes their fear. Now describe where your fear lives.

_____

_____

_____

If you were to draw a picture of your fear, what would it look like? How big is it? What color? What shape? Is it abstract? Draw a picture of your fear in the space provided.

Worksheet

What Does Your Fear Say?

List as many of its statements as you can. This is especially important because it is often what fear says to you that prevents you from taking action toward what you really want. Once you learn what fear typically says to you, you can learn to talk back! Some people's fears say things like, "You'll be sorry! Don't do it! You can't! You'll fail".

My Fear Says:

_____

_____

_____

How Does Your Fear Taste?

Be as descriptive as you can. Rather than saying, "bad," try to be more precise. For example, "my fear tastes as bitter as a 50 mile an hour wind whipping in my face on a 30 degree Vermont winter morning."

My Fear Tastes like:

_____

_____

_____

How Does Your Fear Smell?

Again, be as descriptive as you can. For example, "The smell of my fear is noxious and clinging, like smoke clinging to fabric long after a fire is over".

My Fear Smells like:

_____

_____

_____

By completing these questions you may discover that your fear is not as awful as you first thought it was. On the other hand, if it is truly a monster, now that you can see it clearly, you will be able to cope with it more effectively. The unknown is always more frightening than the known. You'll just make your fear known to yourself.

Letting Go is Scary

Fear occurs when you live in the future instead of the present—when you worry about what might happen. Look at the fears you listed above. Aren't they each related to something that might happen in the future? They are not present-moment realities.

Yet, to get to the future we also need to let go of the present. Fear is an emotion that accompanies the process of letting go. It is a sign that you are growing! The more attached you are to what you have, who you are, what you believe today, the more fear you will experience.

If you are invested in believing that you are smart, bright, and quick to understand, then you will probably experience fear at the invitation to grow into areas in which you have little knowledge. You'll need to let go of being knowledgeable and take on the role of learner. But if you're attached to your self-image, you will be afraid of becoming a student. If you're attached to your view of yourself as in control, you will be afraid to let go of control. Being vulnerable and trusting someone else will scare you. If you are attached to your good paying job, you will be afraid to let go--to try work that promises more fulfillment.

Growth is a continuing process of going beyond. It is not rigid; it is flexible. It changes. To find and fulfill your purpose, you will be called to let go of where you are and go beyond. Of what must you let go, to move closer to your passion?

What Scares You About Letting Go?

Worksheet

What I Need to Let Go of:	My Fear About Letting Go:

When will you feel fear? Usually at moments when you are about to stretch yourself towards new growth. It is a sign that you are entering a personal frontier. It is associated with uncertainty as well as a sense of adventure. There is risk involved. You have an opportunity to move beyond yourself. If you are not feeling fear before you do something, it is an indication that the task at hand is not big enough for you. Think of fear as a reassuring signal that you are on the right course!

Responding to Your Fears

How do you usually respond to your fears? Do you try to eliminate them? Overcome them? Deny them? Avoid them? Worship them? Befriend them? Research them? Ignore them? Talk about them? Take action?

Take a minute now and record three times in your life when you felt afraid.

Situation #1:	
The Fear:	How I Coped:

Situation #2:	
The Fear:	How I Coped:

Situation #3:	
The Fear:	How I Coped:

Based on these three situations, I see that I tend to respond to fear by...

_____

_____

_____

_____

Befriend Your Fear

Fear is not your enemy! If you befriend fear, it can be an asset to you. There is a tremendous amount of energy associated with fear. You have undoubtedly heard stories of people who showed super-human strength when they were faced with fear. Studies have shown that students who felt some fear about taking a test performed better than students who felt no fear. Your goal is not to eliminate fear, but to **harness** it.

Let fear be a catalyst for your growth!

Fear can be transforming or it can be constricting. You decide which one it will be for you. If it is to be transforming, you need to identify what you are afraid of and then look behind it for the growth that is trying to break through. Focus your attention on your goal and let go of where you are.

To support this transformation, it is important to focus on what you want, *your goal*, rather than your *fear*. Then your goal, rather than your fear, will become your motivator! Use the energy that fear produces to take specific action steps that will bring you closer to your goal.

Paradox: To Eliminate Fear, You Must Embrace It.

Worksheet

List your fears about following your passion in the left hand column of the chart below. In the center column, write down what you want—your goal. In the third column, write down the action steps you should take to achieve your goal. An example is completed to help you get started.

Fear	Goal	Action Steps
Example: People won't buy my book	To write a top ten bestseller	Write six hours every day

For many people fear leads to being stuck, to settle for what **_is_** rather than what is **_possible._** You cannot find your purpose; much less fulfill it, without befriending your fears.

Prescription For Fear:

Develop Courage and Take Risks

"Courage is not the absence of fear, rather it is the ability to take action in the face of fear".

Nancy Anderson, *Work With Passion*

There is a skill associated with befriending fear, and that skill is risk-taking. Like any skill, you get better at it with practice. How comfortable are you with risk-taking? Complete the following questionnaire to find out. For each question, answer Yes or No.

Worksheet

Y	N	Risk Questionnaire
☐	☐	1. I don't take as many risks as others might because I know my limits.
☐	☐	2. I seek others approval before I take a risk.
☐	☐	3. I believe it's better to be safe than sorry.
☐	☐	4. I need to feel in control of most situations.
☐	☐	5. If some action scares me, I stop doing it.
☐	☐	6. I take a risk only if there's nothing to lose.
☐	☐	7. I feel uncomfortable with uncertainty.
☐	☐	8. I prefer to do things the way I've always done them.
☐	☐	9. I hate to make a mistake or to be wrong.
☐	☐	10. I think things change too quickly.
☐	☐	11. I research any risk before I go forward with it.
☐	☐	12. I feel uneasy around people who take a lot of risks.
☐	☐	13. I have trouble acting on what I believe.
☐	☐	14. I change my mind easily if other people disagree with me.
☐	☐	15. I can't remember the last time I took a risk.
☐	☐	16. I sometimes wish I had taken a risk in a situation.
☐	☐	17. The first thing I consider before taking a risk is what could go wrong.
☐	☐	18. I have difficulty asserting myself.

The more yes answers you have, the less of a risk-taker you are. If you have more than nine "yeses", this section will help you increase your risk-taking behavior.

Risk Taking

There are three kinds of risk-taking behavior:

Non Risk-Takers.

These people like to play it safe in all situations. If you fall into this category, you answered the risk questionnaire with at least 12 "yeses". Non risk-takers are unlikely to know their passion because to know it would demand they take some action. Not knowing is much safer. If they do become aware of their passion, they complain about why they can't fulfill it. Complaining is safer than being responsible for their lives. Chances are that if you are a non risk-taker you feel powerless over your life.

Calculated Risk-Takers.

These people take planned risks. They consider the possible benefit as well as the probable consequences of an action. They weigh their alternatives before they act. They see mistakes as a learning opportunity, not a failure. They want to grow and stretch themselves. Calculated risk-takers recognize that there are no guarantees and plan accordingly. Even as they go forward with a risk they have a "Plan B" in mind in the event that things don't go as they hoped. They are not afraid to acknowledge when they make a mistake. Because of their careful planning, they often do not perceive their action as a risk.

Bold Impulsive Risk-Takers.

These people love the thrill of a risk! They like to live dangerously. They do not consider the downside of a risk. They wear blinders and see only the outcome they want. Often, the important people in their lives felt uneasy with their actions. For impulsive risk-takers, the sense of danger is what gives them satisfaction, not achieving a specific outcome. If you answer <u>no</u> to all of the questions in the risk questionnaire, you may be an impulsive risk-taker.

Daily Risk Behavior

Before you take the big risks in life, you need to experience success with smaller risks. Take a moment now and record some of the risks you have taken in the past week. These do not need to be major, life changing risks. Remember, you need to start small. If you can't think of five in the past week, list five in the past month.

1. _____

2. _____

3. _____

4. _____

5. _____

Did you have trouble making a list? To increase your risk-taking behavior heed the following advice, "Stretch yourself to be uncomfortable every day." Let's look at how you might do this.

You could:
- Drive a new route to work.
- Say hello first to people you meet on the street.
- Smile at strangers.
- Tell the truth sooner.
- Apologize when you are wrong.
- Compliment people when they do something you like.
- Call someone you don't know but would like to meet and suggest getting together.
- Tell someone you love, "I love you."
- Say something silly.
- Risk being embarrassed.

- Ask what a word means when someone uses language you don't understand.
- Do nothing for a half an hour.
- Speak out at a meeting.
- Express how you feel.
- Disagree with someone.

Worksheet

Using this list as a starting point, write down at least five ways you can stretch yourself to be uncomfortable in the coming week. Then do it! As you do, you will find yourself able to take bigger and bigger risks. At crucial moments of choice, most of the business of choosing is already over. If you don't learn to be a risk-taker today, you won't be able to take a risk when you are faced with a big opportunity. Your moment will pass because you were not ready.

Risks I Will Take...

1. _____

2. _____

3. _____

4. _____

5. _____

Steps to Improve Your Risk-Taking

Step 1:   **Start small.** As your comfort level increases, so will the size of your risks.

Step 2:   **Collect as much information as possible about the possible risk.**

Step 3:   **Consult with other people.** Note that this is different than seeking their approval.

Step 4:   **Ask yourself, "What is the best possible outcome?"**

Step 5:   **Ask yourself, "What is the worst possible outcome?"**

Step 6:   **Ask yourself, "How likely is the worst possible outcome?"**

Step 7:   **Ask yourself, "If the worst possible outcome occurred, what would I do?"** If you don't have an answer for this question, this may not be a risk you want to take.

Step 8:   **Ask yourself, "What is the probable outcome of not taking the risk?"** You may have forgotten that continuing to do what you are doing can be very risky. Your present course is not safer simply because it's familiar. For example, you may be considering changing jobs and thinking your new position is risky. But if you suffer from headaches or some other physical ailment in your current work, you may be risking your health if you don't make a change!

Step 9:   **Evaluate the outcomes of the risks you take.** Did it turn out as you expected? If not, why not? What have you learned for the next time?

Step 10:   **Celebrate your success.** When you take a calculated risk and you achieve the outcomes you wanted, give yourself credit for taking a risk. Gradually, you will come to see yourself as a risk-taker.

Mask #5: What Is Success?

What Is Success?

"Under the values that will guide this more temperament time, the hunger for more will certainly not vanish, but it can be redirected. More money, more tokens of success – there will always be people for whom those are adequate goals, but those people are no longer setting the tone for all of us. There is a new sort of more at hand: more appreciation of good things beyond the marketplace, more insistence of fairness, more attention to purpose, more determination truly to choose a life, and not a lifestyle, for one's self."

Lawrence Shames, The Hunger for More

What is your definition of success?

_____

_____

_____

Describe three achievements in your life. Be specific about what you did, what you achieved, and what there was about the experience that made you decide it was a significant achievement.

Achievement #1:

_____

_____

_____

Achievement #2:

_____

_____

_____

Achievement #3:

_____

_____

_____

What is the relationship between how you define success and your achievements? Do you consider yourself successful?

Lifestyle or Life?

The decade of the eighties was a decade of greed. Life was characterized by more, more, and more, and measured by price tags and designer labels. What you did was less important than how much you were paid for doing it. Choosing meaningful work was less important then choosing work that paid well. Enjoying life took a backseat to having a lifestyle. Success was measured in dollars: your net worth determined your self worth. Materialism, consumption, having things all took the place of the inner work that is necessary for a life of meaning.

Are there any ways in which your lifestyle has taken on more importance than you life?

1. _____

2. _____

3. _____

People got confused. They thought that having things would make them happy. When they obtained these things, there were two rude awakenings. First, having doesn't make you happy. The advertisers promised that when you had a particular car or lived in a particular neighborhood or dressed in a certain way you would be happy. They lied. ***Happiness is an inside job.*** It comes from being who you are, fulfilling your purpose, and living your values. "Things" are empty sources for meaning.

What have you wanted, that once you got it, didn't give you the joy, satisfaction, or happiness that you expected?

1. _____

2. _____

3. _____

Secondly, things are not guaranteed. You can lose them. Thousands of people lost their jobs during the eighties, during the mergers, downsizing, and with the onset of changing technology. In 2000, many more lost their jobs in what is commonly referred to as the dot-com bust. When the jobs went, so did the lifestyles they were collecting. Others lost things when the stock market crashed in 1987. The realization dawned on people that things are transient; they can be taken away. Things are not a stable basis upon which to stake your happiness.

When are you the happiest?

1. _____

2. _____

3. _____

4. _____

5. _____

Did your answers have anything to do with material possessions? The more disconnected and alienated you are from yourself, your inner purpose, the more inclined you are to look outside yourself, like material things, for meaning. As Matthew Fox wrote in *The Original Blessing*, "It is not letting go of things that is important, but the letting go of attitudes towards things."

Having, Do, or Be?

Erick Fromm wrote in *To Have or To Be?* about a misconception that climaxed in the eighties. He said people spent their lives trying to:

HAVE enough "money, resources, and things" so that they can

DO what they want [in terms of work, how they spend their time], because then they can

BE happy.

Unfortunately, most people get stuck at the first step. They never have "enough". Perhaps you've said to yourself, "When I have the car paid off, I'm going to make a change." Then when the car is paid off you said, "After I have the kids educated, then I am going to make a change." One day you reach the end of your life and realize you've never done what you wanted to do with your life.

Fromm says that to have a satisfying life you need to invent the formula. First you need to:

Be who you are. Know your strengths, weaknesses, and your purpose. This self- awareness will lead you to:

Do what you love to do. This doing will be the contribution of your unique gifts. Because you are giving yourself away, you will be rewarded, and

Have what you need. Of course, there are no guarantees you will have everything you want!

As Dick Leider says in *The Power of Purpose*, "There are two ways to be rich; one is to have more, the other is to want less." To reach the stage of having requires patience. While you wait, you need to define yourself by who you are, not what you have.

How do you turn the *having/doing/being* cycle around? You stop making "having money", the goal. You stop measuring success by your bank account and possessions. You get you priorities in order and follow your heart, guided by your values.

Misconceptions About Money

1. Money is the goal.

When money becomes the goal, as it has for so many people, it signals the corruption and deep loss of self. Life becomes trivialized. No amount of money or possessions can ever make you whole. Only living from your center can do that. Money is a reward for services; it is a by-product of excellence; it is a by-product of you passion.

2. Money can make you happy.

Joy and happiness are feelings that come from the inside. They cannot be bought or possessed. These feelings come from a state of being, not of having. You can feel unhappy if you do not have enough money to meet your central needs, but money is not sufficient to give you happiness. "This fascination of simply making money wears thin in time. The real fruits of ones labors are seen in the planning of one's gifts."

3. Money is what makes the world go round.

Sometimes it seems that way! Love, not money, is the true world currency.

4. Once you have enough money, then you can do what you want.

The having mode is very addictive. Your definition of what "enough" is continually rises. Have you noticed that even before you get a salary increase your lifestyle is out ahead of it?

5. Money equals success.

"Making money is a private affair, but success, so to speak, is by general consent; we define it every day. We have a right to demand a real accomplishment, a making of something better, before we give someone our regard and our applause.." Money is a by-product of success.

6. Money makes you powerful.

Money gives you options, not power. Real power comes from within. It is an energy you share with others. Power that comes from outside can be easily lost if others withdraw their support. Because of the addictiveness of the having mode, it is easy to begin taking more than you give. When that happens, the very people who put you in power can take you out of power. Even well-to-do people can feel anxious and uneasy if they lack a center.

7. Money makes you free.

Money is usually spent on possessions. Think for a minute about what you have done with your money. Are you surrounded by things that you need to care for, keep clean, and keep safe? Consumption becomes a trap, not a freedom.

Prescription For The Having Mode:

Shift To The Being Mode

The having mode is certainly seductive. But by definition, having is possessing, and it can disappear as easily as it came. The being mode is not so transient. In this state you are centered, authentic, connected to your spiritual self. You have your personal power to assist you in creating and fulfilling your passion. If you can comfortably be yourself, "without living from your *Shoulds*, then your need for outside approval disappears.

From the centered place of being, your vision of who you are can express itself. You will be drawn to your passion. In the having mode, you feel driven. It is no coincidence that you hear about being "market-driven", or even "value-driven". These concepts come out of the having mode. The language of purpose is "value-led" or "customer-led". What feels better to you, being led, or being driven?

Think back over times when you have felt inspired – times when you were drawn to a person or idea. Recall situations in which you thought to yourself, "I'd like to make that kind of impact." When you felt inspired you may have noticed that you reacted physically with shivers up your spine, or with tears of awe. Describe three situations when you felt inspired.

1. _____

_____

_____

2. _____

_____

_____

3. _____

_____

_____

As you reflect on those situations, were you pulled to take any action? Your passion can be an inspiration to you if you let it be.

Qualities of Being

It is difficult to understand what it means To Be. We spend more of our time doing or having. As you review the following list of being qualities, put a (√) beside the ones you have experienced. Put and (X) in the box beside the qualities you would like to develop.

	Experienced	Develop
1. **Discipline**. A discipline is something you do everyday, whether you feel like it or not, without concern for where it is getting you. To commit yourself to a discipline puts you on the path of mastery and excellence. Examples of discipline can include keeping a journal, meditating, doing what you say you are going to do, playing an instrument, or practicing martial arts. Discipline is not something you have, discipline describes who you are. Your state of being will grow with discipline. As you cultivate solitude, the prescription for Mask #1, you will simultaneously develop discipline.		
2. **Responsibility**. You are responsible to your purpose; to bring it into reality. This is not a responsibility for, but a responsibility to. Your ability to respond comes directly from this state of being. To be yourself requires action; it is not a passive state.		
3. **Be Yourself**. Can you be with yourself quietly, alone? If you cannot be with yourself, you probably don't accept yourself. And if you can't be with yourself, how can you let anyone else be? You will have to spend time and energy changing them. Most importantly, if you can't let yourself be, you will find it extremely difficult to express your being, your passion.		

4. **Present To The Moment**. Being occurs only in the now, this moment. To be demands that you stop living in either the past or the future. When you are in the moment, you are open to life as it unfolds. This present awareness allows you to see and take advantage of opportunities as they present themselves. When you are able to stay in the now you will notice you feel less fear and experience less stress.		
5. **Awareness**. Do you say, "I have a problem?" or do you say, "I feel troubled?" The second phrase is from a state of being. You are aware of how you feel. You are aware of yourself in relation to the rest of the world. Rather than possessions you experience, you are aware of your experience. When you think in terms of having or possessing, the next logical step is to control, conquer, or overcome. Today our relationship with the environment is a classic example of the negative effects of possessing in relating to the world.		
6. **The Observing Self**. Ironically, as you increase your awareness, it is important to stay more present to the moment and develop the other qualities of being. You will discover that you have a level of consciousness that observes all of this. Even as you read and complete the exercises in this workbook, if you are attending, there is a consciousness, the external I Am.		
7. **Vision**. Your passion is an expression of who you are. No one else can be you better than you. Your unique expression in the world comes from being yourself. If you begin the search for your purpose by asking what pays well, you will miss your potential for vision. The more you are able To Be, the more clarity you will have about your purpose.		

Who Are You?

Answer this question twenty times. Resist the temptation to answer the question with what you do or what you have. Try to stay in the being mode.

I am...

1. _____

2. _____

3. _____

4. _____

5. _____

6. _____

7. _____

8. _____

9. _____

10. _____

11. _____

12. _____

13. _____

14. _____

15. _____

16. _____

17. _____

18. _____

19. _____

20. _____

What Is Your Purpose?

Now that you have worked through the five masks, your purpose may be very clear. If it is not yet completely clear, you undoubtedly have a better idea of what it is, and you know which areas (masks) you need to continue working with so that your purpose does become clear. Be patient with yourself!

Write out your personal statement of purpose as you now understand it in the box at the bottom of this page. You might want to include the following parts in your statement:

First, use a verb to describe your purpose. (serve, teach, train, write, create, council, make, sell, etc.) Then choose a noun to describe who or what (children, the elderly, consumers, the earth, the poor, computers, etc.) For the next part, include the skills or talents you will use (you identified these in the exercise in Mask #1). Finally, include the outcome that you want. Here are a couple of examples to get you started:

Example:

1. My purpose is to teach adults how to read, using my love of words, books, and ideas, so that people will be more confident in their day to day living.

2. My purpose is to strengthen families using my counseling skills to help adults be better parents.

Notice that the same purpose can be expressed in many ways. This allows for the growth and change that will occur throughout your life. Thus, a purpose of teaching could change over time from adults to employees at XYZ Company to volunteers at ABC Agency. Even the purpose itself could change. Remember what Matthew Fox said in the quote at the beginning of Mask #4, "… we are called to let go sometimes of past prophetic calls and to immerse ourselves in new ones."

My Purpose Is . . .

Worksheet

In the box, draw a symbol for your passion as you understand it at this moment. There are no right or wrong answers. If your passion remains unclear at this moment, simply draw what comes to mind.

```


```

Now, describe what you drew. If you need help with this, go back to the early sections where passion was likened to a flame. Then fill in your description.

My passion is like

_____
                                            (what you drew)

because_____
                                            (explain)

Part 3

New Truths in a

Life Guided By Purpose

Passion doesn't come from business or books or even a connection with another person. It is a connection to your own life force, the world around you, and the spirit that connects us all. You are the source.

Jennifer James, *Success is the Quality of Your Journey*

New Truths in a Life Guided by Purpose

The secrets for success are well known: drive, persistence, focus, self image, setting and attaining goals, attitude, initiative, enthusiasm, self confidence, time management skills, personal organization and perseverance.

The secrets for finding your purpose are not as well known. You might think of the secrets of success as being the "old truths". The secrets of living your life "on purpose" are the "new truths". The new truths include: process, trust, intuition, paradox, ecology, creativity, levels of truth, patience and flow. In this final part of the workbook three of the new truths will be explored: process, intuition and paradox.

From Goals To Process

> "The tragedy of life doesn't lie in not reaching your goal.
> The tragedy lies in having no goal to reach."
>
> Benjamin Mays

You have been told over and over that reaching the goal is what counts. Goals, in fact, do count but for a goal to count, it must align to your purpose. Some believe the destination is the ultimate aim. But have you ever noticed that reaching that goal doesn't always bring you the joy and satisfaction that you had expected? Look back at the exercise you completed in Mask #5. There you listed examples of goals that didn't bring you the satisfaction you expected.

Goal attainment can be shallow if it is not in alignment with your purpose because it is the process of accomplishment that gives life meaning. It is the striving, the searching, the seeking, and the yearning that is the thrill! It is not the arriving. A goal simply sets the direction, and that's all it is intended to do. If you mistakenly put all your focus on the end result, you will miss your life! Rather than being present to the moment, you will have lived your life in the future. Life occurs in the Now...

If you focus on goals exclusively, on those occasions when you do achieve them, you probably won't take time to savor your accomplishment. Instead you'll be rushing on to the next project.

Do you celebrate your achievements?

The Joy That Comes From The Journey

The importance of process was portrayed beautifully in the academy award winning film, *On Golden Pond*. In it, Henry Fonda spent the summer trying to catch a big fish. Over time, he got his grandson, (Doug McKeon) involved in the search for the big fish. They used a variety of baits and tried different times of day and areas of the lake. Finally they caught him. McKeon was thrilled and was ready to have the fish for dinner. But Henry Fonda wanted to let the fish go. He explained to the confused youngster that the joy was in the search to catch the big fish. Having it was not the objective. McKeon finally understood when they released the fish.

As you move from the having mode to the being mode, you shift your focus from goals to process. Very simply, process is the how of things, not the what. How often have you said, "It's not what she said, it's how she said it," or "It's not what he decided, but how he decided it"? The process: the how of our lives, matters a great deal.

> Remember, when you can, that the definition of success has changed. It is not only survival, the having – it is the quality of every moment of your life, the being. Success is not a destination, a place you can ever get to, it is the quality of your Journey."
>
> Jennifer Jones, *Success is the Quality of Your Journey*

Process is not linear. It is circular. You are going to have an opportunity to experience this now by completing a life cycle exercise. Begin by watching an internal movie; *"THIS IS MY LIFE."* Think back to where you were born, your family of origin, first childhood memories, early school experiences, adolescence, first love, high school years, college days, first job, first significant relationship, marriage, children, disappointments, achievements, and relationships with family and friends. Watch your movie until you reach the present moment of sitting here in the moment reading this page.

On the next page is a large circle. At the top is birth and also death. Recalling your *"THIS IS MY LIFE"* the movie, record the significant experience in your life on your life cycle. Try to include 20 to 25 items.

Your Life Cycle

"We shall not cease from exploration, and the end of all our exploring will be to arrive where we started and know the place for the first time."

T.S. Eliot

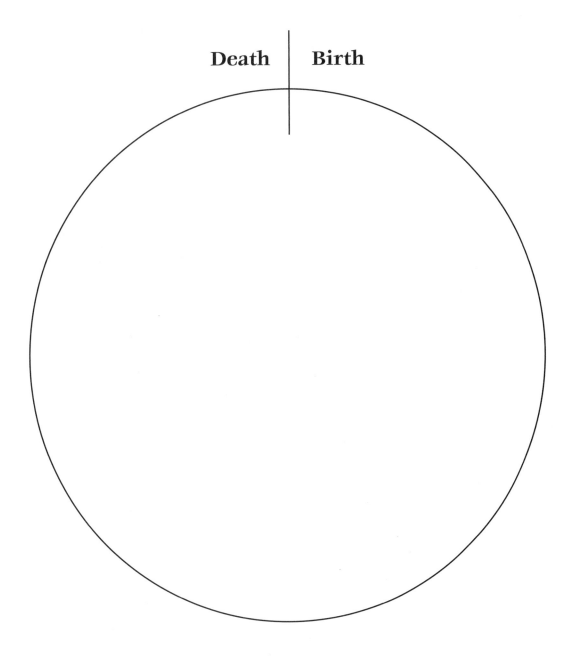

Death | **Birth**

Stepping Stones – Your Life Process

You have just completed a chronology of your life by recording events that have happened during your lifetime period. Now you are invited to get in touch with the process of your life. You are going to take the two dimensional circle and lift it up to become a three dimensional spiral!

Look back at the experiences you recorded. Now go inside yourself and ask, "In a word or two, how would I describe the flow of my life?" In other words, how have you experienced your life subjectively? The objective is to go deeper than the reporting of events, to go to the meaning that they held for you.

For example, two women could each have spent six years at home raising children. But the meaning of that experience can be completely different for each woman. One might describe those years as, "I was trapped," while the other might describe the experience as, "I was nurturing." These process descriptions are a far more intimate expression of your life than a mere chronology.

Another person would know much more about you by listening to the flow of your life than by listening to the chronology of your life. Notice also, that in the example above, a woman might have on her life cycle, "Caitlin born, Scott born, Colin born." Yet, when she thinks about the process, all three chronological events are part of a single event – she either felt trapped by having the children or she experienced strong feelings about mothering and nurturing. This is what is called a stepping stone. As you look at your life cycle, try to remember how you felt. Here are a few more examples to get you started:

"I went to college, was selected to participate in a special intern program, and traveled to another part of the country to study."
(chronology)

"I learned."
(process)

"My husband and I separated and finally divorced."
(chronology)

"I was bitter."
(process)

Your Stepping Stones

Below is a spiral with circles representing stepping stones. Narrow the 20-25 chronological events in your life cycle into no more than ten stepping stones. Write the words that you would use to describe the process of your life on each stepping stone. Try to feel how one process, or stepping stone, flowed into the next. Read through your list of stepping stones quietly to yourself to feel the flow and movement in your life.

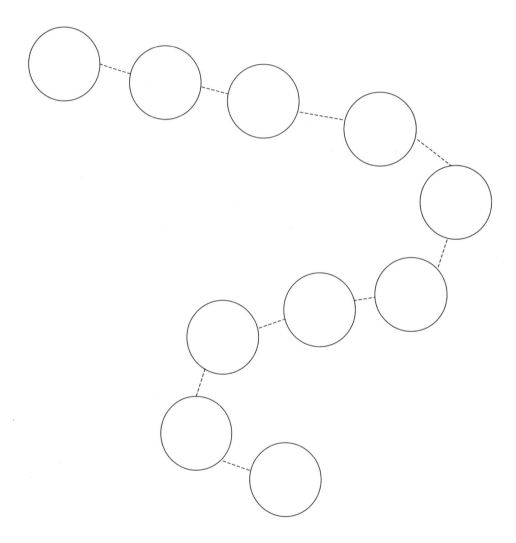

Exploring Your Stepping Stones

Did you start at the top of the page or the bottom of the page as you wrote down your stepping stones? In other words, do you perceive your life climbing or deepening?

Notice the thin line that connects the stepping stones and makes the spiral. This is the common thread that is working its way through your life. Have you allowed each experience to lead you to the next in your life? Can you see that who you are and what you are doing in your life at this moment would not be possible if you had a different set of life experiences? The challenge is to use life experiences as stepping stones and not as bricks that form walls.

The spiral also allows you to see, graphically, the growth process. Before there is movement forward, there is movement backward. In your life, this can feel like you are losing ground or like you are stuck. Such signs are better understood as times of inner growth. Think about the daffodils that bloom in your garden. Before they can flower in the spring, they need a period of dormancy, when it appears that nothing is happening. In fact, the bulb is preparing itself to flower. You are like the flower. You too need a period of time to grow yourself into your next step. Such time can feel dark and bleak.

Process is organic. It demands that you trust yourself and trust something greater than yourself. There is not a moment when your growth is complete; it continually unfolds and flows, until we die. To see life merely as a series of goals is to miss it entirely. To see life with a purpose, the journey is entirely different.

When you shift from goals to process you allow your life to happen instead of trying to control it or to make it happen. To accept your life as an art that is in process demands patience. You need to be able to wait. This is not easy, especially in a culture that demands a quick fix. Solitude, the prescription for Mask #1 will help you to develop patience. Practicing a discipline, as described in the prescription for Mask #5, will also help you develop patience.

You can see that most of your stepping stones encompass a period of months, if not years. Rarely does you life change dramatically from one day to the next. It takes patience to see that the gentle, gradual movement in your life is what enables you to grow. As you trust the process and develop patience, you will dramatically reduce you stress. Finding your purpose is a process that takes time. Reading this workbook in one hour will not give you the answer. This workbook is describing what the process is so that you can have a companion and some guidance on your journey. From soul searching to clarity to action may take some time!

As you look at your stepping stones, notice also that, in order for you to move to the next stepping stones, you need to let go of where you were. You cannot move forward in your growth without being willing to grow beyond where you are. Remember the exercise in Mask #4 on Letting Go? When you have difficulty letting go, your spiral will get larger. At other times you will be aware that your spiral is very tight; change and growth occur quickly then. If you're holding on, growth will be slower than if you take the risk to let go.

Breakthroughs occur when you can let go. Your patience will serve you well here, too. Sometimes you will need to wait before you let go. For example, you may need to put more pieces in place before you quit your current job or whatever your situation may be!

Paradox: **Every act of creation is an act of destruction.**

Internal Time/External Time

Process occurs in a different dimension of time compared to your chronological life. Process functions on internal time, which can be faster or slower than clock time. To get a sense of this for yourself, answer these questions.

When did time seem to fly by? What were you doing? Why do you think it seemed to go so fast?

_____

_____

_____

_____

When did time drag? When did it seem to pass at a snail's pace? What were you doing? Why do you think it seemed to pass so slowly?

_____

_____

_____

_____

When did time stop? When did you totally lose any sense of time? When have you had the experience of the endless **"now"** moment? What was different about this experience from times when time flew or dragged?

_____

_____

_____

_____

Your answer to the third set of questions is a clue to moments when you have been in a state of being, rather than a state of having or doing. Your passion emerges from being and is an expression of your being.

From Logic to Intuition

Most people intuitively know what they want to do. As you worked through the exercises of the Masks you may have noticed that you had a hunch or a gut feeling about your purpose. You may have heard a quiet voice whispering to you telling you what your purpose is. This voice is your "inner knower", or your inner wisdom. Were you listening? Or do you discount this way of knowing?

You will not "figure out" your passion; it is not something that the logical mind uncovers. Your purpose will come to you through another channel, your intuition. At its most developed level, intuition is your connection to a higher level of consciousness. Jung called this the collective unconsciousness. Mystics have called it God. The purpose of removing each of the masks is to enable you to better hear your "inner knower". The new truth is not only to listen but to take action on this knowing period. How often have you said after something happened, "I knew it!"? But you didn't trust what you knew! This level of consciousness is the source of creativity. Intuition is the sixth sense that allows you to know things you could not know with your rational mind.

Every person is intuitive. Many people, however, do not listen.

Worksheet

Take a minute right now to think back over times when your intuition spoke to you and you did not listen. What was the outcome? Do you wish you had listened? Look back and remember three times when you wished you had listened to your intuition.

1. I wish I had listened to my intuition when _____

_____

because _____

_____

2. I wish I had listened to my intuition when _____

_____

because _____

_____

3. I wish I had listened to my intuition when _____

_____

because _____

_____

Blocks to Intuition

Why didn't you listen to your intuition in the examples you just wrote down? It was probably because of distrust, fear, or external listening.

Distrust

To trust your intuition, you need to believe in yourself and trust yourself. The prescription for Mask #3, Developing Self-Esteem, will help you do this. If you aren't confident in your inner wisdom you'll depend too heavily on logic, analysis, and other cognitive, rational processes. There is nothing wrong with the left-brain approach to situations. By itself, however, it does not give you the complete picture. When you trust your intuition, you get more of the truth and you get it much faster than when you use your intellect!

Would you listen to a person you didn't trust? Probably not. In fact, you would actually tune him or her out. The same thing happens when you do not trust your intuition. You drown it out with busy-ness thoughts, analysis, and preoccupations. It is no surprise that some people claim they have no intuition; they've spent years denying, ignoring and distrusting it.

It is uncomfortable not to be able to articulate why you know something or how you know it. That's why intuition requires trust. You need to make a leap of faith and trust that this way of knowing is as valid as any other period. The more you trust your spouse or loved ones the more they tell you about themselves and the better you get to know them. The more you trust your intuition, the better you will get to know it, too.

Intuition also demands your trust because it presents you with pieces. You rarely get all the parts at one time. You need to trust that, as you continue down the path, more pieces will be revealed to you. If you like to be in control, (old truth), this is very difficult!

Fear

Some people try to silence their intuition out of fear. They are not afraid of what their intuition might say but rather that they might need to do something if they listen to their intuition. Once you are aware of what needs to be done, it is hard to respect yourself and maintain high self-esteem if you do not take action. Are you afraid to act on what you know?

You may realize intuitively, after working through the five masks that your passion is in the area of landscaping. If you currently work as an accountant, then you are clearly out of balance with your intuition. To be true to yourself, you need to take some action, no matter how small. Otherwise, your integrity is at stake.

It is so much easier, so much safer, to say to yourself, "I know that I am not happy in my work but I just don't know what to do." Then you can safely "study" the situation. You get ready to know rather than risk knowing.

Worksheet

Be honest with yourself now, what do you know, but hesitate to admit to yourself, because of the action you will need to take?

_____

_____

_____

_____

What scares you about taking action?

_____

_____

_____

_____

External Listening

How often have you discounted your intuition because it didn't agree with what someone else thought? Do you put more credibility in your friends' opinions than in what you intuit? Do you try to meet other people's expectations instead of listening and following your "inner knower"? Do you relinquish your truth for someone else's truth?

To avoid these traps, take action on the prescriptions as outlined in Masks 1, 2 and 3. First, take time alone to know what you want and how you feel (The prescription for Mask #1). Second, identify your values (The prescription for Mask #2), and last, develop your self-esteem so that you can risk being different (Mask #3).

When people in a group withhold their personal opinions to support the opinion of the group, a phenomenon called Groupthink occurs. This is a very dangerous situation for companies, in particular, because without the contributions of individuals, unwise decisions are made and opportunities are missed. When you let someone else dictate the decisions you make about your life, you put *them* in control of your life! When you go along with others without stating your own opinions, you betray your own inner wisdom. Each betrayal is a silencing of your intuition. Eventually, you only listen externally. Internal listening keeps you open to your intuition.

When did you let someone talk you out of trusting your intuition?

_____

_____

_____

_____

How did it turn out?

_____

_____

_____

_____

Developing Your Intuition

There are several steps you can take to develop your intuition. The first is to let go of the blocks to intuition that were just described. Then you can turn up the volume of your intuition by using the techniques discussed below.

Preparation

Your intuition puts pieces together to create a whole, but it needs the pieces to do this. The more information, learning, and experience you gather, the more your intuition has to work with to create an intuitive "flash." True experience is the blending of knowledge, experience, and intuition. For example, if you have been working with computers for the past 10 years, attending conferences, and reading about your field, you will have a better chance of intuitively solving a computer problem than someone who has limited experience, hasn't kept current in the field, and isn't as knowledgeable.

Soil that is well prepared sprouts more seeds than soil that is poorly prepared. Your intuition follows the same principle. The better you prepare yourself, the more your intuition will flourish.

Incubation

When a seed is planted, it needs time to germinate before it sprouts and breaks the soil. We tend to get impatient with this process. We want it now. We try to force it. Intuition cannot be forced; we need to allow it. You have undoubtedly had the experience of trying to solve a problem, but try as hard as you might, no answer came forth. Later, while you were taking a shower or driving somewhere, the answer magically appeared as if from nowhere.

The answer needed time to incubate. After you prepare your mind by giving it everything you know about the problem, you need to give your intuition time to work on it. Assume an attitude of openness to receive the answer your intuition offers.

Aha!

This is the moment of an awareness. The answer comes to you. Sometimes it seems obvious, but other times you may feel uncertain, hesitating to trust what you sense.

Intuition speaks to each person in its own way. Some people report that they experience their intuition as a feeling about something. Others describe a gut reaction. Some see an image or picture of what they need to do or have a dream and still others hear a message.

You need to acquaint yourself with how your "inner knower" communicates with you. This is important, because you can confuse wishes, hopes, and fears with intuition. Each of these is different.

Wishing and hoping are both thoughts. Intuition is not a thought, it is an instant, immediate knowing. There is no rational process.

In Mask #4, you wrote down a description of your fear. You used all five senses – how it feels, sounds, smells, tastes, and looks. Sometimes you may wonder whether your intuition is talking to you, or whether you are just hearing your own fear. You can test what seems to be intuition against what you know is fear.

Worksheet

Think about times when you are aware that your intuition is talking to you.
How does your "inner knower" communicate with you? Be as specific as
possible. Then compare this with how your fear talks to you.

_____

_____

_____

_____

_____

_____

_____

Verification

You need to test your intuition against reality. Try it out and see how it works. You may need to collect more information before you act on your inner wisdom. For example, you might get an intuitive flash to move to another part of the country. Before you sell your home and pack your bags, do some research.

This is true of your passion. Perhaps you're beginning to realize that you want to work with children. Before you quit your present work, investigate the types of work you can do with children, the training you'll need, and so on.

Intuition is at the root of most scientific breakthroughs. Typically, a person may have an intuitive flash about the nature of the universe or about how something works. This is followed by the hard work of verifying the intuitive knowing. Science today is using sophisticated quantum physics to verify the intuitive knowing of mystics who lived centuries ago.

As you begin paying more attention to your "inner knower", it can be valuable to keep an intuition log. First, record whatever you perceive as intuitive flashes or awareness. Then monitor and record how accurate you are in distinguishing intuition from wishes, hopes, or fears. You may discover that what you initially thought was intuition was really a wish. Over time, you will become more skilled at discriminating between your thinking, wishing, hoping, predicting, your fearful self, and your intuitive self. Your intuition log will assist you in better understanding when and how your intuition speaks to you.

Intuition Log

DATE	INTUITION	OUTCOMES

From *Either/Or* to *And*

Our linear approach to life creates dualism (seeing things as either/or). Life, however, is not linear. It is circular. It is a continuing process. Everything cycles back around to itself. Winter and summer are not opposites; one leads to the other. When we realize this, we can see that rather than **_either/or,_ life is _and._**

Learning to see the *and* is not easy. It demands that we become comfortable with paradox. *Either/or* gives us a feeling of certainty and security. *And* is ambiguous and uncertain. *Either/or* limits our thinking; *and* expands it.

Dualism, or seeing things as opposites, creates separation—from ourselves, our work, each other, and our environment. Paradox is about the connections, the unity of ourselves with others, with work, or with the planet. Each way of thinking represents a totally different view of the world.

Science has contributed to dualistic world view, especially in the past few centuries. Newtonian physics presented a mechanistic view of the world in which everything could be subdivided into separate, distinct parts. Over centuries, the search for the smallest building blocks of all matter led to quantum physics. This most advanced form of scientific research has proven that the basic building blocks of everything that exists is a particle and a wave! The essence of life is not *either/or!* It is *and.* Now science leads us into a paradoxical view of the world. These discoveries verify what mystics have been saying since the beginning of recorded history. There is unity and oneness. It is a paradox that we see separation.

The hologram is an excellent example of paradox. It is a two-dimensional object, yet when you look at it, it appears to be three-dimensional. A more common object is a rocking chair. You have undoubtedly sat in one, moving back and forth, back and forth—yet you never get anywhere!

How, comfortable are you with paradox? Paradoxes have been sprinkled throughout this workbook to help you see that finding your purpose is not an *either/or* proposition. It emerges and you create it. It is analogous to the work of a sculptor, who has a vision to create in his/her reality through the medium of stone or bronze. Yet the medium itself will direct the creation. For his sculpture David, Michelangelo accepted a block of marble that had been rejected by previous sculptors because of a deep gash. The stone itself dictated the sculpture, and yet Michelangelo chipped away everything that wasn't

David. From this process came one of the world's most beautiful sculptures.

From a state of being, your intuition will tell you your purpose. The next step is to bring your passion into reality. You become a co-creator as you go about the process of seeing the opportunities in your life to express your passion. The challenge for each of us is to create the vision we see in our hearts.

Worksheet

What follows is a list of paradoxes that apply to your journey. As you read each one, write down your personal experience with the paradox. Here is an example to help you get started.

Example:
The more things change, the more they stay the same.

I felt dissatisfied in my work so I changed jobs. The new company was much better---for a while. Now I feel dissatisfied again. I realize that changing companies wasn't really making a change. I'm still the same!!!!!

_____

_____

_____

To gain control, relinquish it.

_____

_____

_____

To change others, alter yourself.

_____

_____

_____

Every ending is a beginning.

_____

_____

_____

To become a part of, grow apart from.

_____

_____

_____

The soul does not grow by addition but by subtraction.

_____

_____

_____

To become secure, be vulnerable.

_____

_____

_____

The more I learn, the less I know.

_____

_____

_____

Add your own paradox:

_____

_____

_____

You Have One Shot!

Finding your purpose is an inner journey. Only you can answer life's most demanding questions. Here you have a companion to walk you through the process – this workbook, my CDs and my workshops. Let these exercises guide you to deeper levels of awareness. The questions of your purpose will not be answered once and for all. Rather, like the process I described, the answer will emerge as you create it.

The journey you are on is literally your life. Savor it! You only get one shot!

About the Author

By 1991, Jim White, had achieved international recognition as a leadership expert through his work as CEO of Blount World Trade Corporation; Owner and Managing Director of ACEC Centrifugal Pumps NV, Belgium; and as Vice-President and Division Manager of Ingersoll Rand Equipment Corporation. He had also successfully bought and sold 22 companies over two decades. Most of these were companies in trouble that he brought to life as thriving, profitable enterprises—a pattern from his earliest days in business when he made it a point to take on the toughest assignments.

In 1991 Jim founded JL White International, Inc. and **Circle of Success**™--a year-long, customized leadership and management transformation process. This process contains all of the day-by-day systems and techniques he developed and used to transform his 22 companies. Through Circle of Success, he now shows other companies, organizations, and individuals how to create their own unprecedented profit—both professionally and personally.

Jim works with organizations and individuals worldwide, helping them define and implement excellence. CEOs, managers, and entire departments and companies have shown vast improvements through a wide range of customized services that enhance management effectiveness, productivity, and quality of professional relationships.

As a full-service management consulting and leadership development organization based out of Monterey, California, JL White International, Inc. offers a variety of innovative programs. For example, his **Jim White Classic Movie**™ series is a favorite in boardrooms and for management teams and industry associations across the U.S. These one-day workshops use classic movies like *12 O'clock High, Twelve Angry Men, Apollo 13*, and many others to help participants identify various management styles, decision-making processes, corrective action techniques, morale-building methods, and accountability issues. Using movies—a medium everyone loves—makes learning a powerful and memorable process.

YOUR FEEDBACK IS IMPORTANT

What's My Purpose? is the result of over 35 years of making and learning from my own mistakes and from the input from students who have attended my workshops and coaching. My heart felt gratitude to those that have allowed me to be a part of their journey. Your feedback is important to the process! Please take a few minutes to answer the following questions:

The most important ideas for me were:_____

_____

_____

I would like to know more about:_____

_____

_____

I have made the following changes in my life since reading this workbook:

_____

_____

_____

I feel that I am/am not fulfilling my passion. My passion is:_____

_____

_____

Additional comments:_____

_____

_____

Please mail to: **Jim White**
457 Webster Street
Monterey, California 93940
Telephone: 877-647-3103
Fax: 831-656-9423

Or you may email: jim@jlwhiteinternational.com
Website: www.whatsmypurpose.com
                     www.jlwhiteinternational.com